All About Me

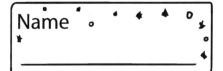

Name

Today is:

I am ___ years old

This is me

My favourite sport

My favourite book

When I grow up I want to be

My favourite meal

My favourite place

My favourite cartoon

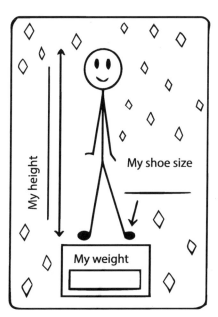

My height

My shoe size

My weight

"Whoever observes fasts during Ramadan out of sincere faith, and hoping to attain Allah's rewards, then all his past sins will be forgiven." (Bukhari)

"Oh you who believe! Fasting is prescribed to you as it was prescribed to those before you, so you may learn piety and righteousness.(2:183)

Ramadan is the 9 th month of the Islamic year and starts after first sighting of the crescent moon.

Fasting means not to eat or drink during daylight hours from before Fajr till Maghrib.

Fasting is a must for all muslims-men, women,kids who have reached adulthood.

"For those who fast, there is a gate in Paradise called Ar-Rayyan, through which no one but they will enter." (Bukhari)

"When Ramadan enters, the gates of Paradise are opened, the gates of Hell are closed and the devils are chained." (Bukhari)

All about Ramadan

A fasting person should keep away from bad behavior and do good deeds.

The fast is not broken if we accidentally eat or drink.

Some people don't need to fast- sick, very old and young kids. However kids can keep fast for part of the day.

Day 1

Color in prayer beads for each Salah you perform today.

Part Half Most Full

Fasting

Color in your fast today.

My good deeds

I read Quran. ☐

I did Zikr. ☐

I gave Sadaqah. ☐

"If Allah desires good for someone, He gives him understanding of the deen." (Bukhari)

My Thoughts

_____
_____
_____
_____
_____
_____

Your Ramadan Train

Let's hop on to the Ramadan train and do a good deed for each day.

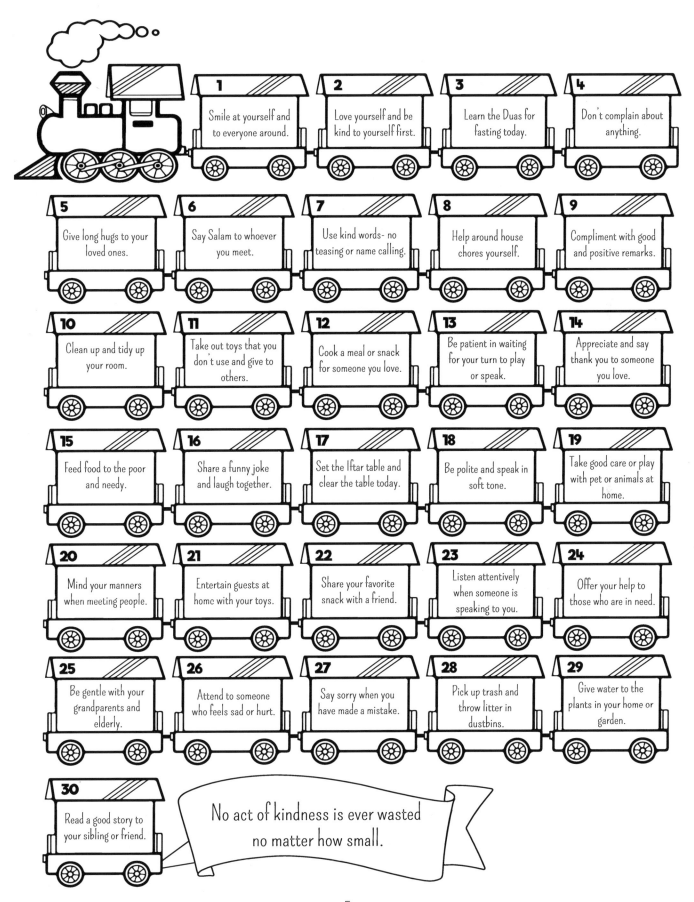

1 Smile at yourself and to everyone around.

2 Love yourself and be kind to yourself first.

3 Learn the Duas for fasting today.

4 Don't complain about anything.

5 Give long hugs to your loved ones.

6 Say Salam to whoever you meet.

7 Use kind words- no teasing or name calling.

8 Help around house chores yourself.

9 Compliment with good and positive remarks.

10 Clean up and tidy up your room.

11 Take out toys that you don't use and give to others.

12 Cook a meal or snack for someone you love.

13 Be patient in waiting for your turn to play or speak.

14 Appreciate and say thank you to someone you love.

15 Feed food to the poor and needy.

16 Share a funny joke and laugh together.

17 Set the Iftar table and clear the table today.

18 Be polite and speak in soft tone.

19 Take good care or play with pet or animals at home.

20 Mind your manners when meeting people.

21 Entertain guests at home with your toys.

22 Share your favorite snack with a friend.

23 Listen attentively when someone is speaking to you.

24 Offer your help to those who are in need.

25 Be gentle with your grandparents and elderly.

26 Attend to someone who feels sad or hurt.

27 Say sorry when you have made a mistake.

28 Pick up trash and throw litter in dustbins.

29 Give water to the plants in your home or garden.

30 Read a good story to your sibling or friend.

No act of kindness is ever wasted no matter how small.

5

Day 2

FAJR ZUHR ASR MAGHRIB ISHA

Color in prayer beads for each Salah you perform today.

Half | Most
Part | Full
Fasting

Color in your fast today.

My good deeds

I read Quran. ☐

I did Zikr. ☐

I gave Sadaqah. ☐

"There are two blessings which many people lose: health and free time."
(Bukhari)

My Thoughts

_____

_____

_____

_____

_____

_____

My Ramadan Goals

Goals are important when you want to accomplish anything in life.
Write down your goals that you want to achieve this Ramadan.

Fasting

Salah

Quran

Others

Day 3

FAJR ZUHR ASR MAGHRIB ISHA

Color in prayer beads for each Salah you perform today.

Part | Half | Most | Full

Fasting

Color in your fast today.

My good deeds

I read Quran. ☐

I did Zikr. ☐

I gave Sadaqah. ☐

"Indeed, Allah will not change the condition of people until they change what is in themselves." (13:11)

My Thoughts

_____

_____

_____

_____

_____

_____

Dua

Dua is our conversation with Allah. It is our special time and communication with our Rabb. We can share all our wishes , wants and needs in our Dua. For Allah loves who make Dua and He loves to give us all that we wish for and He is listening to everything we speak.

We can make Dua in every language, anywhere and at anytime. Allah is our best friend who we can share all that is in our heart and talk to him about anything and everything.

When we make Dua:

We Thank Allah for all the blessings He has given us.

We praise Allah for He is Our Creator who has made us who we are.

We ask for everything that we wish for and we want for ourselves and others.

We share all our troubles and worries with Him so He can make it all better.

We remember all our loved ones and muslims of the world and ask for the betterment of Islam.

Day 4

FAJR ZUHR ASR MAGHRIB ISHA

Color in prayer beads for each Salah you perform today.

Part Half Most Full

Fasting

Color in your fast today.

My good deeds

I read Quran. ☐

I did Zikr. ☐

I gave Sadaqah. ☐

"Truthfulness leads to righteousness and righteousness leads to Jannah. Lying leads to wickedness and wickedness leads to the Fire." (Muslim)

My Thoughts

My Dua List

Talk to Allah! Tell your Creator all that you wish for yourself and for others.
What do you want for yourself? Do you have any requests for your loved ones?
This is the time for your prayers to be answered!
List all your Duas that you want to ask Allah this Ramadan.

Day 5

F A J R • Z U H R • A S R

M A G H R I B • I S H A

Color in prayer beads for each Salah you perform today.

Half   Most

Part   Fasting   Full

Color in your fast today.

My good deeds

I read Quran. ☐

I did Zikr. ☐

I gave Sadaqah. ☐

"He is not one of us who is not merciful to our younger people, nor honours the old among us." (Tirmidhi)

My Thoughts

_____

_____

_____

_____

_____

_____

Suhoor

Suhoor is the time just before the start of Fajr when we eat a meal to keep a fast. It is recommended to have a healthy meal to keep your body nourished and hydrated for the day. Before the sun only begins to rise for the morning, we make intention for fast and then do not eat or drink anything until Iftar time.

What do you like to eat for Suhoor?

"Do Suhoor because in Suhoor there is Blessings."

"Verily, the difference between our fasting and the fasting of the people of the Book is the eating before dawn." (Bukhari)

Day 6

Color in prayer beads for each Salah you perform today.

Part | Half | Most | Full

Fasting

Color in your fast today.

My good deeds

I read Quran. ☐

I did Zikr. ☐

I gave Sadaqah. ☐

"The strong man is not one who is good at wrestling: the strong man is one who controls himself in a fit of rage." (Bukhari)

My Thoughts

Iftar

Iftar is a special time for the fasting person. It is the time when they sit and open their fast upon the call of Prayer at Maghrib when the sun starts to settle down.

Dua at the time of breaking fast

ذَهَبَ الظَّمَأُ ، وَ ابْتَلَّتِ الْعُرُوْقُ ، وَ ثَبَتَ الْأَجْرُ إِنْ شَاءَ اللَّهُ

"Thirst has gone, the veins are moist and the reward is sure, if Allah Wills."

(Dawood)

Fill this table spread with all the food and drinks you like to eat at Iftar. Draw and color in your favourite food on the plates and glasses.

"He who gives food for a fasting person to break his fast, he will receive the same reward as him, and nothing will be reduced from the fasting persons reward." (Tirmidhi)

Day 7

Color in prayer beads for each Salah you perform today.

Fasting

Part | Half | Most | Full

Color in your fast today.

My good deeds

I read Quran. ☐

I did Zikr. ☐

I gave Sadaqah. ☐

"Allah does not look at your body and face, rather,
He looks at your heart." (Muslim)

My Thoughts

Do's/Dont's of Fasting

Fasting is not just about the act of not eating or drinking anything. There is so much more to fasting when we want to please Allah and earn great rewards.

Draw ✔ inside the box for all the acts a fasting person should do and ✗ for all that he or she should not do.

Pray Salah on time.

Always speak the truth.

Speak bad words.

Eat or drink on purpose.

Sleep all day.

Give Sadaqah.

Read Quran.

Learn any Surah.

Be unproductive.

Backbite about others.

Speak lies.

Do as many good deeds.

Show anger.

Stay in a positive mood.

17

Day 8

F A J R ● Z U H R ● A S R
M A G H R I B ● I S H A ●

Color in prayer beads for each Salah you perform today.

Part Half Most Full

Fasting

Color in your fast today.

My good deeds

I read Quran. ☐

I did Zikr. ☐

I gave Sadaqah. ☐

"And whatsoever He created for you on this earth of varying colours. Indeed in this is a sign for people who remember." (16:13)

My Thoughts

_____

_____

_____

_____

_____

_____

Salah

Salah is a must for every muslim to perform regularly. We pray five times a day towards the Qibla of the Kaabah in Makkah.

"The example of the five daily prayers is like that of a clear-water river flowing in front of your houses in which a person washes himself five times a day – cleansing him from all dirt." (Bukhari)

"The key to Jannah is prayer; the key to prayer is Wudu (ablution)." (Tirmidhi)

Mark the timings on the clocks for salah today.

If you want to get the key to Jannah then follow the tips here to open the lock for Jannah.

Do Wudu properly.

Think of Allah while praying.

Be slow in your prayer.

Speak the Ayats for Salah clearly.

Look down at the prayer mat while praying.

Try not to fidget and move.

Do lots of Dua at the end.

 Fajar

 Zuhar

 Asar

 Maghrib

 Isha

Day 9

Color in prayer beads for each Salah you perform today.

Fasting

Part Half Most Full

Color in your fast today.

My good deeds

I read Quran. ☐

I did Zikr. ☐

I gave Sadaqah. ☐

"Ability to act in a calm and composed manner is (a blessing) from Allah, whereas acting in haste is from Satan." (Tirmidhi)

My Thoughts

_____

_____

_____

_____

_____

Allah loves Sadaqah

Sadaqah is anything that a muslim gives to gain Allah's pleasure. It could be food, money, clothes, toys, things or any good deed that you do for the sake of Allah. Even a smile is a Sadaqah. Allah loves those people who give to other people. Let's fill the jar below with all the deeds, things and acts you can think that you will give to others as a Sadaqah to earn Allah's reward.

My Sadaqah

I will smile more often.
I will give away any old books.
I will keep water outside for birds to drink.

"Those who spend their wealth (in Allah's way) by night and by day, secretly and publicly, they will have their reward with their lord." (Quran 2:274)

Day 10

F A J R Z U H R A S R
M A G H R I B I S H A

Color in prayer beads for each Salah you perform today.

Part Half Most Full
Fasting

Color in your fast today.

My good deeds

I read Quran. ☐
I did Zikr. ☐
I gave Sadaqah. ☐

"None of you truly believes (in Allah and His religion) until he loves for his brother what he loves for himself." (Bukhari)

My Thoughts

_____
_____
_____
_____
_____
_____

Fasting is a Shield

"Fasting is a Shield.
Let no one of you during his fasting
day behave in an obscene manner or
become angry.
If anybody fights with you.
Let him say:

I am fasting!"

(Bukhari)

Write in the given shields all the things that we should protect ourselves with when we are fasting.

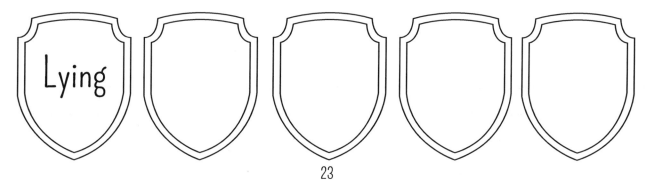

Lying

Day 11

FAJR ZUHR ASR MAGHRIB ISHA

Color in prayer beads for each Salah you perform today.

Part / Half / Most / Full

Fasting

Color in your fast today.

My good deeds

I read Quran. ☐

I did Zikr. ☐

I gave Sadaqah. ☐

"The most beloved actions to Allah are those performed consistently, even if they are few." (Bukhari)

My Thoughts

Pillars of Islam

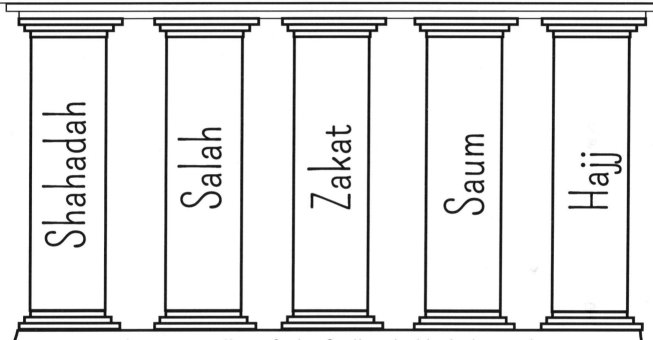

Every building needs strong pillars for its foundation. In Islam, we have five pillars of belief and ritual that we must obey and follow. These are the five duties that every muslim must obey in their life.

Shahadah

Salah

Zakat

Saum

Hajj

Do you know your pillars of Islam? Fill in the blanks here to know more.

Shahadah means to believe that there is no God but _____ and Prophet _____(pbuh) is His last Messenger.

Salah is to pray _____ times a day towards our Qiblah which is the _____ in Makkah.

Zakat is for the needy and _____. Every year, muslims take out a certain amount of their _____ to give to those in need.

Saum means to _____during the month of Ramadan. Muslims don't eat or drink anything during the daylight hours.

Hajj is a special journey to _____ that every muslim must make _____ in their lifetime if they are healthy and have the wealth to support their trip.

Day 12

F A J R ● Z U H R ● A S R
● M A G H R I B ● I S H A ●

Color in prayer beads for each Salah you perform today.

Part | Half | Most | Full

Fasting

Color in your fast today.

My good deeds

I read Quran. ☐

I did Zikr. ☐

I gave Sadaqah. ☐

"Allah alone created the heavens and the earth with truth. Verily!
That is surely a sign for those who believe." (29:44)

My Thoughts

_____

_____

_____

_____

_____

_____

Your Prayer Mat

Design your prayer mat as you want it to be. You can be creative in including ideas from your current prayer mat that you pray on. Use Islamic patterns, designs and color it as you like.

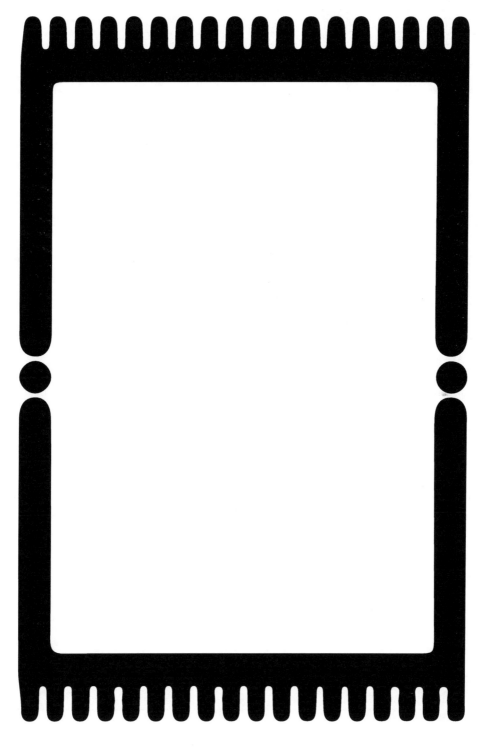

Day 13

F A J R • Z U H R • A S R
M A G H R I B • I S H A

Color in prayer beads for each Salah you perform today.

Half   Most
Part   Fasting   Full

Color in your fast today.

My good deeds

I read Quran. ☐
I did Zikr. ☐
I gave Sadaqah. ☐

"Righteousness is good morality and wrongdoing is that which wavers in your soul and which you dislike people finding out about." (Muslim)

My Thoughts

Manners of Sleep

Prophet Mohammed (pbuh) has guided us with the right bed routine for good sleep.

★ Brush your teeth before sleeping.

★ Make Wudu before going to sleep.

★ Dust your bed three times before lying down on it.

★ Do Zikr and Dua after lying down on bed.

★ Do not sleep on your stomach.

★ Read the Dua for when you wake up from sleep.

★ Sleep on your right side with your right hand under your cheek.

★ If you see a bad dream then make a spitting noise on your left three times. Make Taawuz and change your sleeping position.

Dua before going to bed:

اَللّٰهُمَّ بِاسْمِكَ اَمُوْتُ وَاَحْيٰي

"Oh Allah! by Your name I live and die."
(Bukhari)

Dua after waking up from sleep:

اَلْحَمْدُ لِلّٰهِ الَّذِيْ اَحْيَانَا بَعْدَ مَآ اَمَاتَنَا وَاِلَيْهِ النُّشُوْرُ

"All praise be to Allah, who gave us life after killing us (sleep is a form of death) and to Him will we be raised and returned".
(Bukhari)

Day 14

FAJR ZUHR ASR MAGHRIB ISHA

Color in prayer beads for each Salah you perform today.

Half Most

Part Full

Fasting

Color in your fast today.

My good deeds

I read Quran. ☐

I did Zikr. ☐

I gave Sadaqah. ☐

"Allah will not show mercy to him who does not show mercy to others."
(Bukhari)

My Thoughts

Islamic Months

The 12 Months:

5: Jumadi-ul-Awwal   جُمَادَى الْأُوْلٰى

6: Jumadi-uthani   جُمَادَى الثَّانِى

7: Rajab   رَجَبْ

1: Muharram   مُحَرَّمْ

2: Safar   صَفَرْ

3: Rabiul-Awwal   رَبِيْعُ الْأَوَّلْ

4: Rabi-uthani   رَبِيْعُ الثَّانِى

8: Sha'ban   شَعْبَانْ

9: Ramadan   رَمَضَانْ

10: Shawwal   شَوَّالْ

11: Zhul-Q'ada   ذُوالْقَعْدَهْ

12: Zhul-Hijja   ذُوالْحِجَّهْ

What is the 9th Islamic month?

_____

What is the 1st Islamic month?

_____

Write the Islamic months in the correct order:

1)_____

2)_____

3)_____

4)_____

5)_____

6)_____

7)_____

8)_____

9)_____

10)_____

11)_____

12)_____

31

Day 15

FAJR ZUHR ASR MAGHRIB ISHA

Color in prayer beads for each Salah you perform today.

Part Half Most Full

Fasting

Color in your fast today.

My good deeds

I read Quran. ☐

I did Zikr. ☐

I gave Sadaqah. ☐

"Indeed Allah will admit those who believe and do good deeds to gardens beneath which rivers flow." (22:23)

My Thoughts

_____

_____

_____

_____

_____

Our Super Heroes

Allah has given many super powers to His Prophets. How well do you know the Super Heroes of Islam?
Match the super miracle granted to the right Prophet by Allah.

PROPHET	SUPER MIRACLE
Prophet Moosa	He could cure the blind and the lepers.
Prophet Dawood	He got swallowed by a fish and still came out alive.
Prophet Ibrahim	He used his staff to turn into a Serpent which ate up all the smaller snakes of the Pharaohs magicians.
Prophet Mohammed	He could understand the language of the birds, insects, animals and talk to them.
Prophet Isa	He could soften iron with the use of bare hands.
Prophet Sulaiman	He could not burn. The fire became cool for him.
Prophet Yunus	He was given the most sacred book of guidance for all mankind.

Day 16

F A J R Z U H R A S R M A G H R I B I S H A

Color in prayer beads for each Salah you perform today.

Part Half Most Full

Fasting

Color in your fast today.

My good deeds

I read Quran. ☐

I did Zikr. ☐

I gave Sadaqah. ☐

"When a servant of Allah tells a lie, an angel goes a mile away from him."
(Tirmidhi)

My Thoughts

A Blessing to Mankind

Holy Quran is a true blessing for all of us. It teaches us how to live our lives in this world. It tells us about our past. How well do you know your Quran? You can choose from the words below.

The first verses of the Quran were revealed to Prophet Mohammed (PBUH) in the cave of _____

The Quran was revealed over a period of _____ years.

The first word revealed to our Prophet Mohammed (pbuh) was_____which means to _____.

Surah _____ is the first surah of the Quran.

Quran also talks about angels which are Allah's special creation and are made of _____

There are 114 _____ in the Qur'an and is divided into 30 sections.

Quran is a _____ for all Mankind from the time of the Prophet until the day of Judgement.

Prophet _____ was told by Allah to build an ark for his followers.

Allah has _____ the Qur'an. It has never been changed and never will.

A _____ is a person who knows the whole Qur'an by heart.

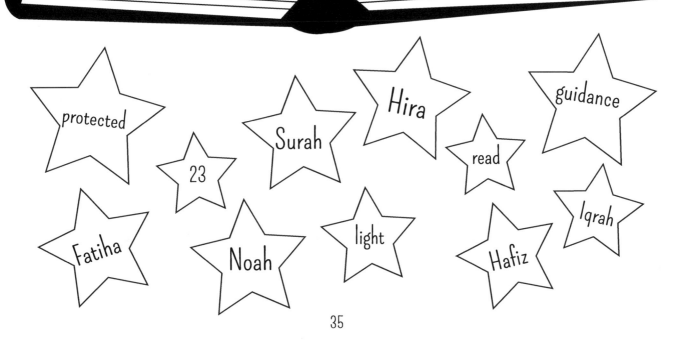

protected

23

Surah

Hira

guidance

read

Iqrah

Fatiha

Noah

light

Hafiz

Day 17

FAJR ZUHR ASR MAGHRIB ISHA

Color in prayer beads for each Salah you perform today.

Part Half Most Full

Fasting

Color in your fast today.

My good deeds

I read Quran. ☐

I did Zikr. ☐

I gave Sadaqah. ☐

"Who has created the seven heavens one above another.
You can see no fault in the creation of The Most Merciful." (67:3)

My Thoughts

_____

_____

_____

_____

_____

_____

Fruits of our Quran

" Do you not see that Allah sends down rain from the sky, and We produce thereby fruits of varying colors?" (Quran 35:27)

Figs "By the fig and the olive" (Quran 95:1)Prophet(pbuh) mentioned figs and said: "If I had to mention a fruit that descended from Paradise, I would say this is it, because fruits of Paradise do not have pits." (Bukhari)

Bananas "And banana trees layered with fruit." (Quran 56:29)

Grapes "Would any of you like to have a garden of date-palms and grapevines, through which running waters flow, and have all manner of fruit therein." (Quran 2:266)

Dates "Whoever takes seven Ajwa dates in the morning will not be affected by magic or poison on that day." (Bukhari)

Pomegranate "It is He Who has brought into being gardens, the trellised and untrellised and the palm trees,and crops,all varying in taste, and the olive and pomegranates, all resembling one another and yet so different." (Quran 6:141)

Olive "He causes to grow for you the crops,olives, palm trees, grapevines, and every kind of fruit Indeed in that is a sign for people who give thought." (Quran 16:11)

Allah has created all fruits for our pleasure and taste. Pick one of these fruits that you like or any other that you prefer and research about it. You will be amazed about its benefits for yourself.

I like to eat _____ because _____

_____

_____

Day 18

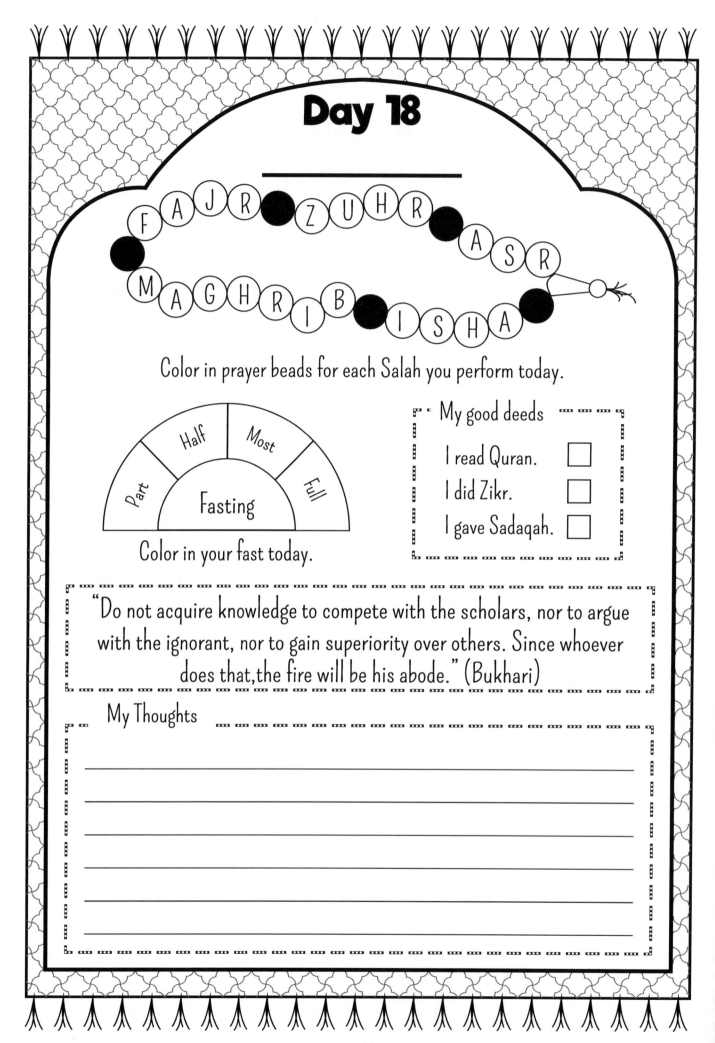

FAJR ZUHR ASR MAGHRIB ISHA

Color in prayer beads for each Salah you perform today.

Part Half Most Full

Fasting

Color in your fast today.

My good deeds

I read Quran. ☐

I did Zikr. ☐

I gave Sadaqah. ☐

"Do not acquire knowledge to compete with the scholars, nor to argue with the ignorant, nor to gain superiority over others. Since whoever does that, the fire will be his abode." (Bukhari)

My Thoughts

Find Our Prophets

Allah has sent Prophets to mankind to pass His messages of worship to all beings. From time to time, there have many prophets sent to earth. Let's find their names below:

K	M	U	S	A	U	E	Z	X	H
P	L	X	K	T	I	S	H	A	Q
Z	M	O	H	A	M	M	E	D	L
Y	N	G	R	D	O	F	Y	B	I
A	S	U	L	A	I	M	A	N	B
Y	F	Q	R	M	T	K	V	U	R
A	U	H	G	S	I	I	J	H	A
Q	I	S	M	A	E	L	S	M	H
U	Y	O	U	N	U	S	P	A	I
B	W	Y	O	U	S	U	F	O	M

ADAM	YOUSUF	IBRAHIM	ISA
ISHAQ	ISMAEL	MOHAMMED	MUSA
NUH	YOUNUS	SULAIMAN	YAQUB

Day 19

F A J R · Z U H R · A S R
M A G H R I B · I S H A

Color in prayer beads for each Salah you perform today.

Half   Most

Part   Fasting   Full

Color in your fast today.

My good deeds

I read Quran. ☐

I did Zikr. ☐

I gave Sadaqah. ☐

"Recommend help to the needy and you will get
the reward from Allah." (Muslim)

My Thoughts

_____

_____

_____

_____

_____

_____

Spot the Differences

Here are two pictures of father and son praying taraweeh but there are 10 differences between the two pictures below. Can you find all of them?

Day 20

FAJR ZUHR ASR MAGHRIB ISHA

Color in prayer beads for each Salah you perform today.

Part Half Most Full

Fasting

Color in your fast today.

"It is better to sit alone than in company with the bad; and it is better still to sit with the good than alone." (Bukhari)

My Thoughts

The Night of Power

During Ramadan, there is one special _____ called Laylatul Qadr. This night is also called "The Night of _____ as this one night is greater than a thousand months. This means that when we do one good _____ in this night, we get the same reward as doing the deed every night for over a thousand months.

On this night, the _____ was brought down to the lowest heaven from the "Lawh-i-Mahfooz". We don't know when the exact _____ of this special night is but we do know that it is during one of the odd nights in the last ten days of Ramadan.

In today's _____, people have shorter lives in comparison but Allah has given us this golden ticket of this special night Laylatul Qadr so we can

X _____ our rewards by praying in the odd nights of the last ten days of Ramadan. We should spend this night by reciting the Quran, performing _____ doing _____ of Allah and doing as many good deeds as possible. Whoever _____ in prayer on the night of Al-Qadr seeking Allah's forgiveness and hoping for His reward sincerely, Allah will forgive him of all his sins.

Find the words from below and fill in the blanks above:

Salah   Zikr   time   date   Quran   deed   multiply   stands   night   power

43

Day 21

Color in prayer beads for each Salah you perform today.

Fasting

Part | Half | Most | Full

Color in your fast today.

My good deeds

I read Quran. ☐

I did Zikr. ☐

I gave Sadaqah. ☐

"Exchange gifts as that will lead to increasing your love for one another."
(Bukhari)

My Thoughts

_____

_____

_____

_____

_____

_____

Laylatul Qadr Dua

"Whoever performed Salat at night in it with sincere faith and hoping for a reward form Allah, then all his past sins will be forgiven." (Bukhari)

Best Dua to pray in these nights:

اَللَّهُمَّ اِنَّكَ عَفُوٌّ ، تُحِبُّ الْعَفْوَ فَاعْفُ عَنِّي (Tirmidhi)

Write the correct letter from the source code below to reveal the meaning of the Dua.

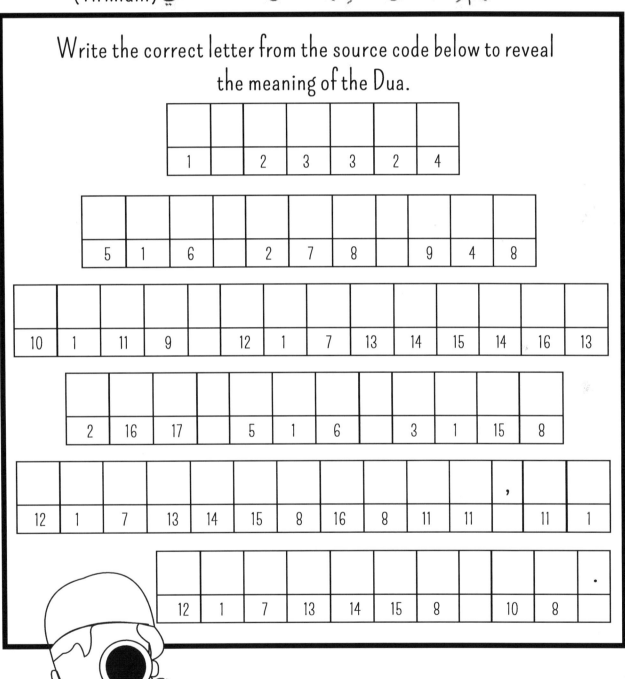

1		2	3	3	2	4

5	1	6	2	7	8	9	4	8

10	1	11	9	12	1	7	13	14	15	14	16	13

2	16	17	5	1	6	3	1	15	8

										,		
12	1	7	13	14	15	8	16	8	11	11	11	1

								.	
12	1	7	13	14	15	8	10	8

Source Code

1	2	3	4	5	6	7	8	9	10	11	12	13	14	15	16	17
O	A	L	H	Y	U	R	E	T	M	S	F	G	I	V	N	D

Day 22

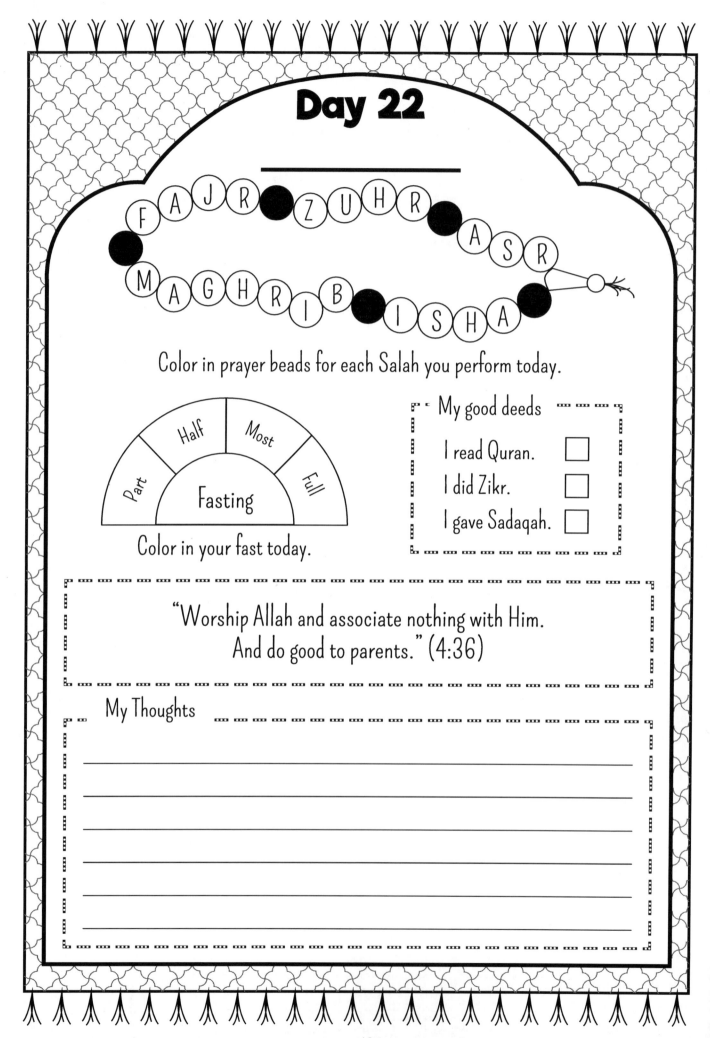

Color in prayer beads for each Salah you perform today.

Half | Most
Part | Full
Fasting

Color in your fast today.

My good deeds

I read Quran. ☐
I did Zikr. ☐
I gave Sadaqah. ☐

"Worship Allah and associate nothing with Him.
And do good to parents." (4:36)

My Thoughts

Taraweeh

Taraweeh is a salah prayer that is prayed in the nights of Ramadan. It is performed between the Isha prayer and the Witr Salah.

Taraweeh comes from the word Tarweehah, which means "rest". In this prayer the imam and the people stand in congregation and recite Quran for a long time and then sit down and rest after every four Rakah.

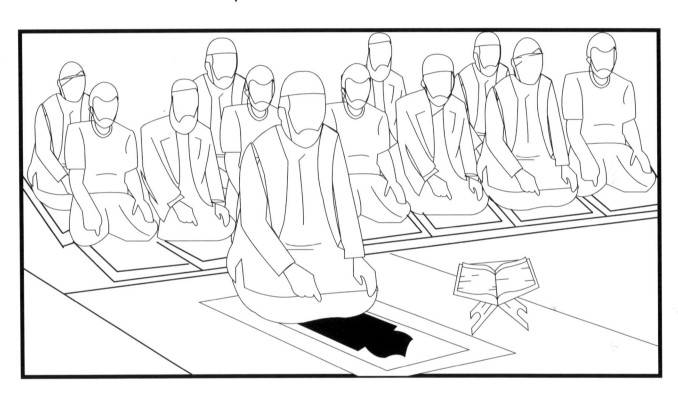

"Whoever offers the night prayers during Ramadan with firm belief and the hope of reward from Allah will be pardoned of all his past sins." (Bukhari)

How can you make your Ramadan more rewarding from Allah?

Day 23

Color in prayer beads for each Salah you perform today.

Half · Most · Part · Full

Fasting

Color in your fast today.

My good deeds

I read Quran. ☐

I did Zikr. ☐

I gave Sadaqah. ☐

"Whoever helps his brother in his time of need,
Allah will be there in his time of need." (Muslim)

My Thoughts

99 Names of Allah

Asma ul Husna are the names by which Allah (swt) refers to Himself in the Quran. Our beloved Prophet (pbuh) said:

"Allah has 99 names. Whoever memorizes and embraces these qualities will enter heaven." (Bukhari)

Rearrange the letters to reveal some of the names of Allah and then draw a line to match their meaning.

	Name of Allah	Meaning of Name
Al-AFGRHF	Al-Ghaffar	The One
Al-LIMKA	Al- _____	The All Able
AL-QAHQ	Al- _____	The King
AL-QKHLIA	Al- _____	The Ever Forgiving
AL-RISBA	Al- _____	The Creator
AL-DIHA	Al- _____	The All Seeing
AL-RBAR	Al- _____	The Guide
AL-HADA	Al- _____	The Truth
AL-RIQAD	Al- _____	The Most Kind
AL-WDUDA	Al- _____	The Loving

Day 24

Color in prayer beads for each Salah you perform today.

Fasting — Part, Half, Most, Full

Color in your fast today.

My good deeds

I read Quran. ☐

I did Zikr. ☐

I gave Sadaqah. ☐

"If someone eats or drinks forgetfully then he should complete his fast, for what he has eaten or drank, has been given to him by Allah." (Bukhari)

My Thoughts

_____

_____

_____

_____

_____

_____

Complete the Masjid

Let's complete the masjid by following the design on the grid on the other side.
You may use a scale to be more accurate and colour it at the end.

Day 25

F A J R Z U H R A S R
M A G H R I B I S H A

Color in prayer beads for each Salah you perform today.

Part · Half · Most · Full

Fasting

Color in your fast today.

My good deeds

I read Quran. ☐

I did Zikr. ☐

I gave Sadaqah. ☐

"Avoid that which I forbid you to do and do that which I command you to do to the best of your capacity." (Bukhari)

My Thoughts

_____

_____

_____

_____

_____

_____

Our Creator Allah

"He is Allah, the Creator, the Inventor of all things, the Bestower of forms. To Him belongs the Best Names. All that is in the heavens and the earth glorify Him. And He is the All-Mighty, the All-Wise." (Quran 59:24)

Allah created everything and everyone. He created all the things we can see and all that we cannot see also. He alone has the power over everything. The more one knows about Allah, His Creations and His Attributes, the more one will love Allah and have hope in Allah. Can you think of some of the things that Allah has created?

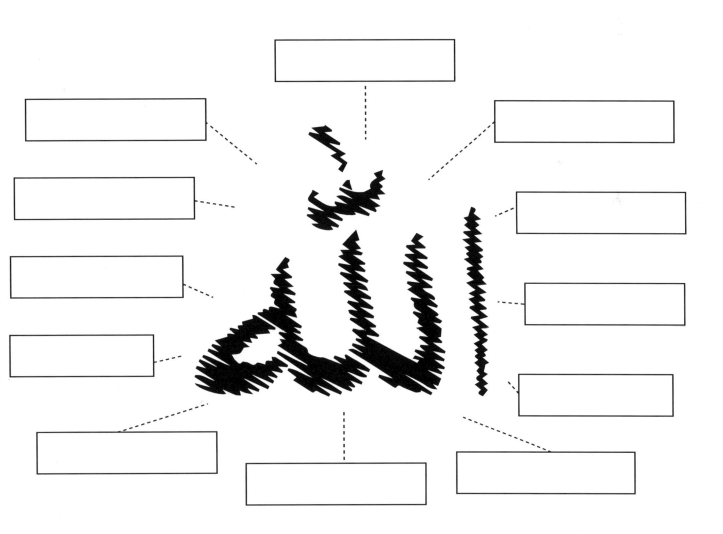

Day 26

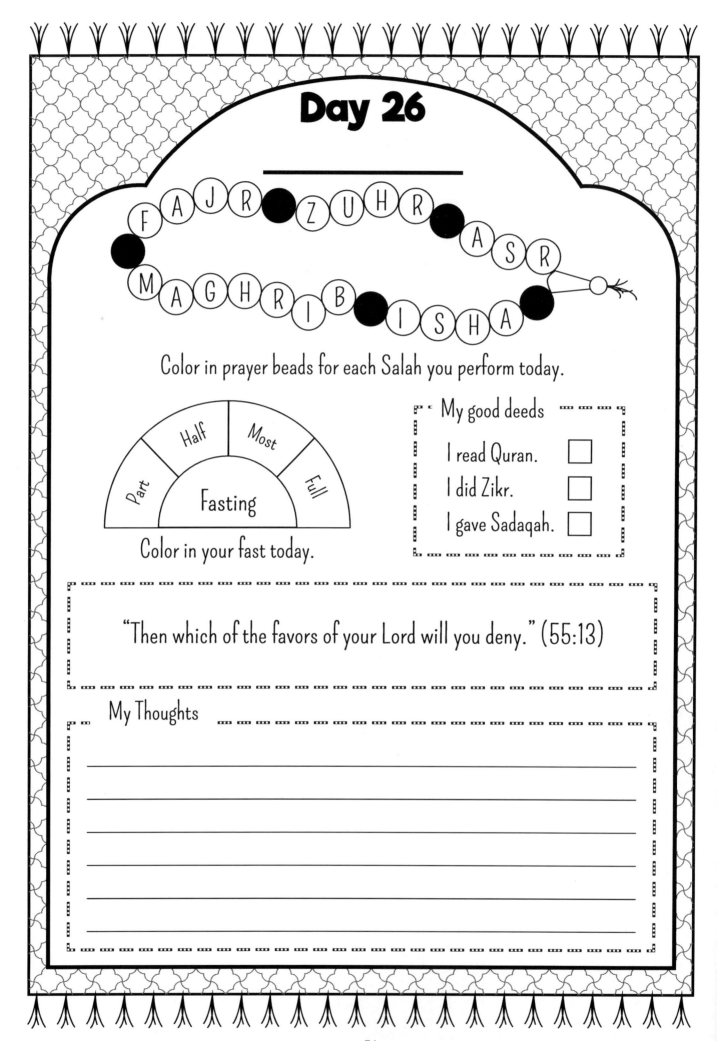

FAJR ZUHR ASR MAGHRIB ISHA

Color in prayer beads for each Salah you perform today.

Part Half Most Full

Fasting

Color in your fast today.

My good deeds

I read Quran. ☐
I did Zikr. ☐
I gave Sadaqah. ☐

"Then which of the favors of your Lord will you deny." (55:13)

My Thoughts

_____
_____
_____
_____
_____
_____

Islamic Crossword

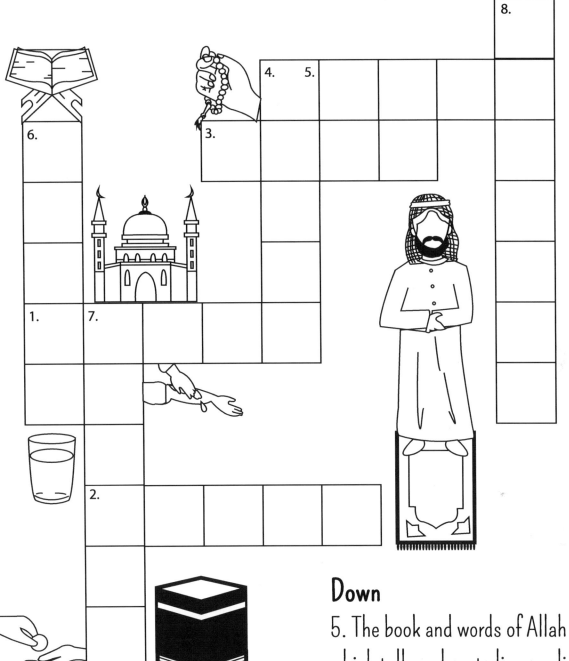

Across

1. It is the Islamic call to prayer.
2. A form of charity that is given to the needy during the month of Ramadan.
3. It is the procedure of wiping parts of the body to purify for prayer.
4. The direction of the Kaaba to which muslims turn to prayer.

Down

5. The book and words of Allah which tells us how to live our lives.
6. A practice of prayer in Islam and is also one of the pillars of Islam.
7. The name of the well that has been giving water to people since years and is located within Masjid Al- Haram.
8. It is a form of Zikr by repeating Ayats to glorify and praise Allah.

Day 27

FAJR ZUHR ASR MAGHRIB ISHA

Color in prayer beads for each Salah you perform today.

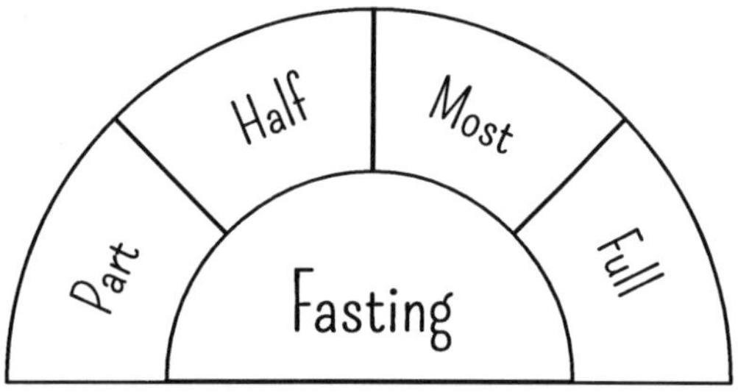

Part Half Most Full

Fasting

Color in your fast today.

My good deeds

I read Quran. ☐

I did Zikr. ☐

I gave Sadaqah. ☐

"If a Muslim plants a tree or sows seeds, and then a bird, or a person or an animal eats from it, it is regarded as a charitable gift (sadaqah) for him." (Bukhari)

My Thoughts

_____
_____
_____
_____
_____
_____

Time to go to Masjid

Help this family through the maze to reach to the Masjid to pray Salah on time.

Day 28

Color in prayer beads for each Salah you perform today.

Part | Half | Most | Full

Fasting

Color in your fast today.

My good deeds

I read Quran. ☐

I did Zikr. ☐

I gave Sadaqah. ☐

"Who is the most excellent among the Muslims?" He said, One from whose tongue and hands the other Muslims are secure." (Bukhari)

My Thoughts

Connect the Quran

Day 29

Color in prayer beads for each Salah you perform today.

Part | Half | Most | Full

Fasting

Color in your fast today.

My good deeds

I read Quran. ☐

I did Zikr. ☐

I gave Sadaqah. ☐

"And it is He who created the night and the day,
and the sun and the moon." (21: 33)

My Thoughts

Thank you Ramadan

Our blessed month Ramadan has come to an end. Let's write an email to a friend to tell them all that you have learnt during this time. Share your experience of keeping fast, giving charity and doing all the good deeds. You can also send a drawing of your choice which can show your feelings of achieving so much during this pious month.

SEND

To:

From:

Subject:

Day 30

Color in prayer beads for each Salah you perform today.

Fasting

Part · Half · Most · Full

Color in your fast today.

My good deeds

I read Quran. ☐

I did Zikr. ☐

I gave Sadaqah. ☐

"Those who spend their wealth by day and night, in secret and in public, they shall have their reward with their Lord." (2:274)

My Thoughts

_____

_____

_____

_____

_____

_____

Eid Mubarak

Ramadan takes us on a journey for purification of our soul, body and faith. The end of the month of Ramadan is celebrated with Eid Ul Fitr.

Eid is marked by giving Sadaqat ul Fitr which is in the form of some grain or money given to the poor by the elders of the house on behalf of the whole family. We wear our best clothes and offer Eid prayers in the morning. Everyone greets each other with happy smiles and says "Eid Mubarak" to all.

How do you plan to spend the Eid days with your family?

_____

_____

_____

"May Allah guide us and our children
to the Straight Path and grant us the
love and knowledge of our Islam."
Ameen

♥Made with lots of Duas and Love for our children.♥

JazakAllah for all the efforts:
Ali Khawaja
Madiha Arif
Zoha Khawaja
Aaminah Habeeb

info@ramadanjournal.org
Ramadanjournal.org

Printed in Great Britain
by Amazon